CAMPING

CAMPING

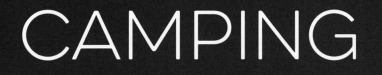

ODYSSEYS

NATE FRISCH

CREATIVE EDUCATION

Published by Creative Education
P.O. Box 227, Mankato, Minnesota 56002
Creative Education is an imprint of The Creative Company
www.thecreativecompany.us

Design by Blue Design (www.bluedes.com)
Production by Joe Kahnke
Art direction by Rita Marshall
Printed in China

Photographs by Alamy (Daily Mail/Rex, Design Pics Inc.,
imageBROKER, Montgomery Martin, mauritius images
GmbH, Radius Images, Jack Sullivan, Leon Werdinger),
Creative Commons Wikimedia (Albert Bierstadt - BOCA
Museum of Art, Les Stroud/Gear Junkie), Getty Images (John
Springer Collection, Jeff Vanuga), iStockphoto (DoraDalton,
Onfokus, Pekic), The McManus Comedies (Derrick King),
Monthsofediblecelebrations.com (Trail Cookery for Girl
Scouts/Home Economics Department of the Kellogg's
Company), Shutterstock (Mikael Damkier, daseaford, Daxiao
Productions, Greg Epperson, Gemini78, Jens Ottoson, varuna,
Rob Wilson)

Library of Congress Cataloging-in-Publication Data
Names: Frisch, Nate, author.
Title: Camping / Nate Frisch.
Series: Odysseys in outdoor adventures.
Includes bibliographical references, webography, and index.
Summary: An in-depth survey of the history of camping,
as well as tips and advice on how to adapt to unexpected
situations, and the skills and supplies necessary for different
types of camping.
Identifiers: LCCN 2016031798 / ISBN 978-1-60818-685-3
(hardcover) / ISBN 978-1-56660-721-6 (eBook)

Subjects: LCSH: 1. Camping—Juvenile literature. 2. Camping—
History—Juvenile literature.
Classification: LCC GV191.7.F75 2017 / DDC 796.54—dc23

CCSS: RI.7.1, 2, 3, 4, 5; RI.8.1, 2, 3, 4, 5; RI.9-10.1, 2, 3, 4; RI.11-12.1,
2, 3, 4; RH.6-8.1, 2, 4, 5; RH.9-10.2, 4, 5

First Edition 9 8 7 6 5 4 3 2 1

CONTENTS

Introduction 9

Camping to Live, Living to Camp 11

Making Sense of Tents 22

Extreme Luxury or Extreme Simplicity 25

Low-Risk Practice 32

Adapting to Nature .39

Footing the Bill 47

Camping from the Couch. 53

Comedic Camping 58

Mind over Matter 66

A Mini Sleeping Bag Model 72

Glossary 77

Selected Bibliography 78

Websites. 79

Index 80

Introduction

Adventure awaits! It's a call from Mother Nature heard by nature lovers and thrill seekers alike. This temptation beckons them, prompting them to pack their gear, pull on their jackets, and head out the door. From mountain peaks to ocean depths and everywhere in between, the earth is a giant playground for those who love to explore and challenge themselves. Not content to follow the beaten

OPPOSITE: Yosemite Falls in California's Yosemite National Park provides a picturesque setting for adventure seekers. National parks offer many options for people who want to explore the beauty of nature by day and camp out at night.

path, they push the limits by venturing farther, faster, deeper, and higher. Going to such lengths, they discover satisfaction, excitement, and fun. Theirs is a world of thrilling outdoor adventures.

Camping is among those adventures. Dating back to the time of early humans, it is now an activity for casual recreation—or life-or-death survival. People have come to associate camping with various topics of drama, humor, and suspense. This has made it a popular subject in literature, television, and movies. Today, camping is accessible to people from nearly all walks of life. However, only a small percentage possesses the skills, equipment, and desire to take camping to harrowing extremes.

Camping to Live, Living to Camp

Camping is usually defined as recreational time spent outside a home or other permanent structure. But thousands of years ago, a campsite *was* a home. Compared with most animals, humans were slow and weak for their size. They didn't have fur for warmth. Their skin was too thin and soft to offer protection. Their senses of smell and hearing were poor, and they could not see well at night. Humans had to rely on their intelligence to survive.

Evidence of tool use by **hominids** dates to 2.6 million years ago. Rocks were selected to break down tough foods and possibly to strike animals for food or defense. Tool technology eventually included shaped stones and wood with sharp edges. Later on, tools were made by combining multiple items.

These advancements allowed early humans to better hunt and gather food during the day. At night, they could make shelters by cutting, breaking, and arranging **foliage** or rock. The first fires were started as far back as 400,000 years ago. By about 125,000 years ago, most humans knew how to light and maintain fire.

As a portable, controllable source of warmth, fire allowed people to live in colder regions. This meant they could hunt the larger game often found in those places. Fire could then be used to cook the meat, making it easier to eat. The flames also helped scare away large predators that had an inborn fear of fire.

As many more thousands of years passed, the basic model of human existence remained the same around the world. Tools were used for acquiring and cooking food and for building and maintaining shelters. A "campsite" would be used only as long as conditions remained suitable. When it was time to leave, the people would gather up their few belongings and move on.

Starting around 12,000 years ago, the domestication of plants and animals began to change the human way of life. Growing crops and raising livestock decreased the need for travel. People could build homes that were more secure and weatherproof than the temporary sites of the past. Living in one place also allowed people to acquire more possessions.

For cultures that adopted this settled lifestyle, camping as a way of life came to an end. But this transition was not a fast one in North America. Within the past 150 years, many American Indian tribes still followed the seasonal migration patterns of the animals they hunted. The portable camps of Plains tribes are among the most noteworthy. Their bison-hide tepees inspired the designs of many modern tents. What ultimately ended the mobile

BELOW *Emigrants Crossing the Plains* shows early settlers in covered wagons traveling across the United States. Albert Bierstadt was on an expedition in 1863 when he saw the wagon train headed for Oregon. He painted it six years later.

lifestyle of most tribes was the arrival of other camps.

European explorers came first. They used boats and horses to carry camp supplies over long distances. Settlers followed in covered wagons. These might be considered the first recreational vehicles (RVs), as they carried supplies and served as a nighttime shelter.

Many of those settlers became ranchers. Long cattle drives gave rise to stories of cowboys sleeping beneath starry skies. Of course, they also faced a lot of poor weather. Many cowhands relied more on the quality of their hats and slickers than they did on any sort of shelter.

Later in the 1800s, army camps began spreading across America in efforts to "tame the West." When a unit stopped its march, white canvas tents would go up. The soldiers did not necessarily enjoy this form of lodging, but there were often no alternatives. Tent camps have been used by armies throughout recorded history. For many military forces, they are still a reality today.

Other campers of the late 19th century included people whose jobs took them to more remote areas. Trappers, loggers, miners, and anyone else who made a living off natural resources needed to follow those resources. This meant moving from place to place as the resources dried up.

While some campers were dedicated to exploiting nature, others were devoted to exploring it. These included expeditions in the areas that would become Yellowstone, Yosemite, and Grand Canyon national parks. As is often true of camping trips, things did not always go according to plan. Group members got lost, boats full of supplies sank, and weather caused delays. Nonetheless, these expeditions signaled the future of camping because they helped people see the importance of preserving wild places.

Natural areas began earning government protection and public appreciation in the early 1900s. Around the same time, some of the first true recreational campers began spending their days and nights out in nature. In 1910, the Boy Scouts of America organization was established. Among its earliest and lasting activities was camping.

Whether for personal fulfillment or research, many 20th-century explorers scaled mountains and sought hard-to-reach places. Such undertakings often required shelters and equipment that were durable but also easy to carry. For several decades, camping mostly remained the domain of explorers, armies, and natural resource harvesters and managers. It was not until the 1970s that camping as casual recreation really blossomed in

America. After the turbulent 1960s, in which the United States was divided over issues of racial inequality and war, people seemed ready to unwind. But the country was also experiencing economic hardships. The search for inexpensive recreation led many people to camping. Campers would hike, picnic, swim, play games, and fish during the day. Then they'd make s'mores around the fire before climbing into sleeping bags at night.

Tent manufacturers of army-style or expedition tents began selling family tents and compact backpacking tents. And as the economy recovered in the 1980s, RVs and camper trailers became popular luxury items. The early 2000s saw another period of economic trouble accompanied by another surge in camping. Today, camping in its various forms remains an accessible pastime regardless of one's location, income, age, or fitness level.

Some campers keep "pee bottles" in their tents on cold nights. That way, they can "go" without exiting their tent and losing vital heat. The warm containers can then become heat sources inside sleeping bags.

Making Sense of Tents

Initially, budget-priced tents may look similar to pricey **three-season** tents. However, the cheaper tents aren't as tough and don't handle varying weather conditions as well. Their rainflies are often flimsy, undersized, and block air flow and trap condensation. The rainflies of higher-quality tents are more durable and provide fuller coverage. They usually lie a few inches above the tent body to allow air to circulate through the tent, even during rain showers. Also, inexpensive tents typically have seams along the bottom edges of the floor, making them susceptible to leaking in heavy rain. Pricier tents often have bathtub-style floors with seams several inches off the ground. The poles of cheaper tents are usually fiberglass or rigid aluminum, which can break more easily than the flexible aluminum alloy poles packaged with most high-end tents.

Extreme Luxury or Extreme Simplicity

Camping can be categorized many ways. Among the simplest is to sort campers by the equipment they use. The farthest removed from extreme campers are those who roll into campsites with an RV or camper trailer. Many of these hook up to electric and water utilities. The most luxurious even come with kitchens, restrooms, air conditioning, beds, and couches. Therefore, this type of

OPPOSITE: An RV or camper trailer provides many of the comforts of home, no matter where you park. But a tent offers campers a more intimate experience with nature and wildlife.

While tenters can camp alongside RVs in many campgrounds, there are countless places tenters can go that RVs can't.

camping basically requires the same skills and materials needed for maintaining a home. Smaller RVs, trailers, and pop-up campers may lack kitchen and restroom facilities. But they still boast built-in beds that are off the ground and protected by solid roofs and walls.

Tents remain the most traditional and versatile shelter for camping. They vary widely in shape, size, and construction materials, depending upon their purpose. What they have in common is their portability. While tenters can camp alongside RVs in many campgrounds, there are countless places tenters can go that RVs can't.

Basic equipment suitable for any type of tenter

includes matches or lighters. Flashlights or lanterns are handy for nighttime navigation around camp. Various forms of insect repellent are beneficial wherever mosquitoes, biting flies, or ticks are common. Soft foam earplugs can make sleep easier by blocking out the sounds of other people, noisy bugs, or storms. Travel-sized soap, shampoo, and toothpaste can make being in close quarters more pleasant. Quick-drying towels of various sizes are useful for drying oneself and equipment.

For weekend **car camping**, inexpensive tents will offer basic privacy as well as protection from insects and light rain. Low-cost sleeping bags or even bedding from home is adequate for mild summer nights. Bulky air mattresses or cots are feasible so long as there is room to pack them. Insulated coolers allow car campers to bring nearly any food they like, and portable gas camp stoves or charcoal grills work well for cooking meals. A few utensils, dishes, and a small washtub with soap and a rag round out a weekend camping kitchen.

A small percentage of campers spend their nights in more remote **backcountry** areas. These may be found in national parks, forests, and grasslands or in public wilderness regions. Some people seek out such places to escape the stresses and crowds of modern life. For others, making camp is simply a necessity during hiking, hunting, horseback riding, mountain climbing, mountain biking, or canoeing trips.

Backcountry campers usually have to leave behind many luxuries of car camping. This includes anything that requires electricity. At the same time, they often bring a few extra necessities, such as first-aid kits, knives, and toilet paper. Backcountry campers often choose more durable or compact versions of tents, bedding, and other gear. Other specialized equipment varies according to the campers' purposes and mode of transportation.

Hunting parties might establish a base camp that puts them close to the animals they are pursuing. Such campers often favor durability above all else. The steel-framed, canvas-covered "wall tents" found in some camps can measure more than 20 feet (6.1 m) long. They can weigh more than 350 pounds (159 kg). Many are designed to contain a portable woodstove and chimney. They don't have floors, so occupants typically sleep on elevated cots. All-terrain vehicles (ATVs) or pack animals are often used to haul in the bulky equipment.

As for differences between other types of backcountry campers, canoers need boats, paddles, and life jackets, of course. Buoyant, watertight storage will help protect electronic devices and critical equipment. Insect repellent is often essential near wetlands. Bikers have bikes and tools for their maintenance, **mountaineers** may have harnesses and other climbing gear, and hikers may use trekking poles. But for the most part, those campers who travel by canoe, bike, or foot use similar equipment.

Low-Risk Practice

Backcountry camping can be easy when the weather is mild and predictable. It can be another story completely when conditions are unexpectedly severe. Some campers find themselves many miles into the backcountry before realizing that their new tent doesn't shed rain well or that their camp bedding is unsuited to the freezing temperatures. A simple precaution is to give gear and nighttime accommodations trial runs in a backyard or campground near home. Choose some nights that are cold, wet, and/or windy. If would-be campers' equipment can last through these conditions, they are ready for the backcountry. If their gear doesn't hold up to the elements, they can retreat to a house or vehicle. There they can safely consider what changes to make before their next trial run.

Most backcountry campers choose small three-season tents for their versatility in different weather conditions. They typically have built-in floors and can be sealed to keep out rain and wind but hold in heat. Or by opening flaps and vents, they can allow for cooling ventilation. Four-season tents close up even tighter to block out the elements. These tents have the strength to stay upright under heavy winds and loads of snow. But the trade-off for added warmth and strength is more bulk and less breathability, so their use is generally restricted to wintry conditions or snowy mountains.

Shelters with complete frames are referred to as freestanding. Campers who insist upon minimal weight may select non-freestanding shelters, which feature only a pole or two (or sometimes none). Stakes and tie-out lines

Extreme campers don't even use tents. They can find shelter tucked between rocks or under a tree. This hiker spends the night on the summit of Needle Point in the Wallowa Mountains of Oregon.

keep the structure erect. Many of these don't have floors, so campers may use a bivouac sack, or bivy. This is something like a waterproof body bag into which they place their bedding. Some campers forego a tent altogether and use only a bivy. Sleeping bags vary greatly in bulk and warmth. They usually have a temperature rating listed, but that doesn't mean they will be comfortable at that temperature. Campers should pick a bag that's rated about 15 to 20 °F (8 to 11 °C) colder than what they expect to encounter.

Sealed, **freeze-dried** meals are popular among backcountry campers. They can be found at grocery stores, outfitter shops, and some department stores. These meals weigh very little and last for years without refrigeration. But once hot water—heated over a campfire or compact gas burner—is added and absorbed, the food expands

Desserts

COCOANUT MACAROONS

REFLECTOR OVEN
BOWL
FORK OR EGG BEATER
CUP
whites of two eggs
  beaten stiff

½ cup sugar
1 cup shredded cocoanut
2½ cups Kellogg's
    Corn Flakes
salt
½ teaspoon vanilla
2 tablespoons water

Mix all ingredients together. Drop by teaspoonful on a greased pan and bake in a reflector oven until brown, or about 10 minutes.
Yield: 10 servings.

SOME MORES

GREEN STICKS
10 marshmallows

20 graham crackers
20 bars of plain chocolate,
   broken in two

Toast a marshmallow slowly over the coals till brown, then put it inside a graham cracker and chocolate bar sandwich. The heat of the marshmallows will melt the chocolate just enough, and the graham crackers on the outside are nice to hold on to as well as good to eat. Though it tastes like "some more," one is really enough. This recipe may be varied by using slices of apple in place of the graham crackers; by using pineapple slices or peanut butter in place of chocolate.
Yield: 10 servings.

CHOCOLATE DROPS

KETTLE
SMALL STICKS
PIECES OF WAXED
PAPER

1 cup sugar
2 tablespoons cocoa
½ cup milk
20 marshmallows

Make a fudge of the sugar, cocoa and milk, cooking until it forms a ball in water, stirring with a clean stick to keep from sticking. Take from fire; one at a time dip marshmallows, on ends of sticks, into the fudge until they are coated with it. Twist in air, holding over waxed paper or napkin in hand, to catch drips, and eat when cool. The first round will be thinly coated; the next will be coated with thick candy.
Yield: 10 servings.

The recipe for s'mores first appeared in a 1927 Girl Scout book. For backcountry campers who want this treat without carrying bulky marshmallows or melty chocolate, freeze-dried s'mores are available.

into large meals that contain combinations of meat, vegetables, noodles, and rice. Common snack choices include granola and energy bars, nuts, beef jerky, and dehydrated fruit—all of which require no refrigeration and provide energy for staying warm and active.

Fresh water is critical for all campers. Canoers often use filters or water treatment tablets to cleanse the water around them for drinking or food preparation. Boiling water is another way to kill water-borne bacteria and parasites. Mountaineers amidst high peaks may melt snow to drink. Other campers employ these techniques when possible, but natural supplies of water are not always available. As a result, packing in water can be a heavy but vital necessity.

Adapting to Nature

Whether striking off across a rolling prairie, under a dense forest canopy, into a desert valley, through a network of waterways, or up a mountain slope, leaving crowds behind can relieve stress and provide a sense of freedom. But escaping civilization also increases your chances of getting lost and reduces access to medical attention in the event of illness or injury.

The first challenge backcountry campers face is navigation. Global

OPPOSITE: Backcountry campers who stay in a different location each night must pack light so that they can carry all their equipment with them for however long their trip takes.

Before heading into the backcountry, campers should tell someone else where they plan to go and for how long.

Positioning System (GPS) devices provide reliable, accurate means of keeping one's bearings. However, maps and compasses don't rely on batteries. Some cell phones are advertised to provide GPS capabilities. Unlike actual GPS units that receive signals from satellites, though, cell phones get signals from towers, and reception is often nonexistent in backcountry areas. This also means that dialing for help is not a reliable option. Before heading into the backcountry, campers should tell someone else where they plan to go and for how long.

First-aid kits with general pain medicine, antiseptics, and other supplies for treating wounds, burns, and breaks are recommended. A small booklet kept in the kit can guide campers through many common procedures. Antivenoms for snake and **arachnid** bites and stings have a short shelf life and are available at medical facilities only *after* a bite or sting has occurred. Therefore, people in venomous snake, scorpion, and spider territory need to be cautious of where they step, sit, or grab.

Although they don't cause the same immediate alarm as a scorpion, black widow, or brown recluse spider, ticks can spread illnesses such as Lyme disease and Rocky Mountain spotted fever. Symptoms range from headaches to vomiting to nerve damage. If left untreated, they can even be fatal. Ticks generally have to be attached to a host for several hours to pass illnesses on, so checking regularly for ticks can help avoid problems. Wearing bug spray and limiting access to skin by tucking shirts into waistbands and pant legs into socks is recommended in areas where ticks are present.

Contact with plants such as poison ivy and poison oak can result in irritating rashes and blisters. Even people who recognize these plants often step into them accidentally in thick foliage. High socks and long pants are helpful in such places. Campers rummaging for fire-building supplies should avoid touching these plants and must not throw them in a fire. Smoke carries their toxins and can spread them to a camper's face, eyes, mouth, and lungs.

Worse than touching toxic plants is eating them. Consuming poisonous leaves, berries, or mushrooms can result in painful sickness and even death. Some backcountry campers find and eat edible plants and mushrooms without incident, but it is not a good idea to

guess. Campers might also eat fish that they catch while in the backcountry. Fish taken from cold water may be safe to eat raw right away, but cooking it is better. Where permitted, some people also kill, cook, and eat other animals in the backcountry. In a pinch, eating bugs can provide sustenance.

In regions with bears, backcountry campers should do their cooking and meal cleanup 100 yards (91.4 m) or so from where they plan to sleep. Additional food should be hung high and at a safe distance from camp. Some campers in bear territory choose to carry firearms, but many wildlife officials contend that bear spray is more effective. And for campers who travel on foot, cans of bear spray are easier to carry than most guns.

While many of the previously mentioned risks affect only some campers, dealing with changing weather can be a challenge for all. Extreme conditions can be life-threatening, and even moderate changes can make an outing miserable. Selecting a good location to make camp is an important first step in preparing for weather. In places with significant changes in altitude, high elevations are typically colder and breezier than low elevations. Exceptions include valley and canyon floors, where dense cold air settles below warmer air. Water also collects in these areas during heavy or prolonged rain showers. Campers wanting the warmest spots should seek low, sheltered areas while staying 15 to 20 feet (4.6–6.1 m)

above depressions in which cold air and moisture accumulate. Conversely, campers in hot locations may want a higher, exposed site where wind sweeps away excess body heat. Good or bad, breezes coming off large bodies of water are generally cool.

Location aside, a roaring fire can ward off the cold. To get a blaze going, light quick-burning tinder, such as dry leaves or shredded tree bark. Then place it under kindling such as twigs or pine cones. Finally, introduce progressively larger pieces of wood as the flames grow in size and temperature. Fire requires oxygen, so arranging a loose structure works better than tight piles. Rubbing sticks or rocks can create the initial spark needed to start a fire, but matches or various types of lighters are easy to carry and use.

Choices in shelters and bedding also play a major

Footing the Bill

The actions of backcountry campers don't typically create problems for other people. However, campers who become lost, get caught in bad weather, or are immobilized by illness or injury are often helped by Search and Rescue (SAR) teams. SAR may involve helicopters, ATVs, boats, search dogs, and large teams of people, and expenses add up quickly. U.S. national parks spend more than $5 million annually on SAR efforts. People who receive the help generally pay nothing. Searches done in U.S. national forests also require the saved people to pay very little. Instead, the cost is covered by taxes or park admissions. When divided among millions of people, the cost per person is low, but many still believe that those who take the risks should be responsible for paying the bills

Making camp is hard when there is no ground to set things on. Rock climbers on sheer cliffs may spend their nights on hammocks or cots that are suspended from the rock itself.

role in withstanding various conditions. A tent or other shelter can provide shade when hot, retain warmth when cold, and form a barrier against wind and precipitation. Cold-weather sleeping bags are often contoured to one's body. This reduces the amount of space that needs to be insulated. They also have built-in hoods that keep warmth near the head. However, sleeping bags don't insulate well on the bottom side, and contact with the cold ground saps more heat than the surrounding air does. Campers in cold places benefit from insulated sleeping pads.

Sleeping bags and pads don't actually create warmth, so cold-weather campers may perform quick, rigorous exercise or huddle near a fire to get their body temperature up before climbing into their bedding. Loading up on calories during the day also helps fuel the body's natural furnace at night.

For those who don't have man-made shelters or bedding—either by choice or by unexpected circumstance—nature can provide the materials. While many shelter designs exist, most involve making a basic frame from sturdy branches or small trees, and then building up layers of brush until gaps are filled. Angled walls best deflect wind and rain. They also help reflect heat from a fire back to the camper. Thick layers of pine needles create an insulated mattress, and more piled on top can serve as a blanket. Survival booklets show how to build different types of shelters and, along with cordage and a compact tarp, can make shelter construction much simpler.

Camping from the Couch

Although most people are happy that humanity's days of wilderness survival are generally over, human vs. nature conflicts have remained a popular staple in media and storytelling. Many people who will never pitch a tent— much less camp in the backcountry— are nonetheless intrigued by factual and fictional accounts of the unpredictable events that can occur in wilderness camping.

OPPOSITE: Movie adaptations of popular books have helped glamorize the outdoors. In 1935, Clark Gable and Loretta Young starred in *Call of the Wild*, a film based on a novel by Jack London that originally focused more on a dog named Buck.

Since camping itself ranges in type and intensity, the portrayal of camping in literature, movies, and TV also varies a great deal. Among the first works of fiction involving camping is Daniel Defoe's 1719 novel *Robinson Crusoe*. Still popular today, Defoe's novel describes how a sailor is shipwrecked on an island and survives using his wits and the natural materials at hand. In truth, people in many parts of the world were living this way at the time, but to the primarily European readers, the idea was unusual and exotic.

As decades went by, civilized cultures remained fascinated by the daily hardships of those they considered "uncivilized." Factual accounts became even more remarkable than fictional adventure novels. Dating back to the 1800s, the stories of early trappers in the wild American West were published for Easterners. They enjoyed the tales of living off the land, encountering terrifying animals, and weathering blizzards—all from the comfort of their armchairs.

By 1885, author Mark Twain's novel, *Adventures of Huckleberry Finn*, was available in both Europe and America. Unlike most adventure stories that had come before, Twain's book centered on Huck's conscious choice to seek adventure. Twain describes scenes such as Huck on a riverbank cooking fish over a campfire in front of his tent of blankets. Such depictions made camping sound

The Iditarod Trail Sled Dog Race in Alaska covers approximately 1,100 miles (1,770 km). Temperatures can dip to -50 °F (-46 °C). Mushers camp along the trail with no shelter—just bedding and their dogs huddled around them.

Comedic Camping

Regarding tent manufacturers' tendency to overestimate sleeping capacity, Patrick F. McManus joked that one of his tents "was designed to sleep two grown men, providing they were both Pygmies and on exceptionally good terms with each other." From the late 1970s into the 2000s, McManus wrote humorous short stories and observations for magazines such as *Outdoor Life* and *Field & Stream*. He also wrote several books, including *A Fine and Pleasant Misery* (1981). The semi-fictional accounts were inspired by his own experiences in the outdoors, including childhood misadventures in the Rocky Mountains of Idaho, where the grand ideas of McManus and his friends were usually undermined by terrible equipment and a general lack of skill. McManus's clever wording and willingness to poke fun at himself transformed common camping scenarios into hilarious reading.

more appealing to the armchair readers.

In the early 1900s, stories from Jack London were popular. London often focused on the gold rushes of northwest Canada and Alaska and the prospectors and sled dogs that swarmed to those areas. The camps described in books such as *The Call of the Wild* (1903) bustled with activity and excitement for the potential of striking gold. This was a dramatic shift from stories such as *Robinson Crusoe*, in which camp was often lonely and the future held more doubt than promise.

Camping was not limited only to realistic fiction. It was also part of many fantasy adventures. J. R. R. Tolkien's 1937 novel *The Hobbit*, for example, revolved around a troop of adventurers making a long journey through various lands. Many of the most significant events take place at their nightly campsites. An attack of giant spiders

TAKEAWAY

As camping became a popular activity in the 1970s and '80s, its representation in the media changed again.

one night and the sounds of bears scuffling outside on another could very well have been inspired by real-life fears of many campers.

The mid-1900s saw a major shift in media as film technology improved and televisions became common. Westerns were among the popular shows early on, and many included scenes of cowboys or lawmen gathering around campfires at night. They would peacefully lie down on the bare ground with their hats pulled over their eyes. This stood in contrast to many previous depictions of nighttime camps that seemed to always be under threat from natural or even supernatural forces.

As camping became a popular activity in the 1970s and '80s, its representation in the media changed again. Lead characters were no longer just hardened explorers, grizzled men, or ambitious teenage boys. Children's book series such as The Berenstain Bears added stories about camping. TV shows including *The Brady Bunch* featured lighthearted episodes about family camping trips. The 1979 movie *Meatballs* focused on the funny side of youth summer camps. Around the same time, the vulnerability of average people in camp settings provided the basis for suspense or horror films, including *Friday the 13th* (1980).

The late '90s and early 2000s saw a sudden rise in reality TV programming, which put people in various situations without scripts. *Survivor* was one such show.

First aired in 2000, it combined candid human inter-action, game-show elements, and wilderness survival. Audiences enjoyed seeing regular people figure out how to meet their basic needs on unsettled islands or in other remote locations.

TV producers figured audiences might also like to watch survival experts in unscripted situations. In 2005, *Survivorman* showcased Les Stroud, who filmed himself surviving in various remote locations for a week or more with minimal equipment. Stroud emphasized sensible planning and minimizing risk in the process of building shelters, starting fires, and obtaining food. On the other hand was Bear Grylls, star of *Man vs. Wild*. This program depicted less conventional situations and more extreme approaches to overcoming them. Grylls's solutions included turning a dead sheep inside out for

Les Stroud has been filming his experiences in the wild for television audiences since 2005. He has demonstrated his survival skills in places such as the Costa Rican rainforest, Arctic ice floes, and the Sonoran Desert.

use as a sleeping bag and picking half-digested berries out of bear feces to eat.

While these television shows were modeling how to survive in the wilderness, a couple big-screen films emphasized the harsh consequences of camping excursions gone wrong. The 2007 film *Into the Wild* dramatized the story of Christopher McCandless. A young college graduate, McCandless left behind a typical American lifestyle in 1992 for a solo stay in the Alaskan wilderness. He overcame various setbacks as he learned to survive, but eventually he misidentified and ate a poisonous plant. This ultimately proved fatal.

Another true Alaskan tragedy is the story of Timothy Treadwell. The topic of the 2005 documentary *Grizzly Man*, Treadwell considered himself a bear expert. He spent several summers camping in areas where he could be near the massive animals. In 2003, he tried to shoo away an old male bear that was stalking near his camp. The bear attacked and killed Treadwell and his companion Amie Huguenard.

And so by the early 2010s, the portrayal of camping in entertainment media had come full circle. From a necessary battle for survival, to an intriguing component of exploration, to voluntary adventure, to laid-back recreation and amusement, to dark and mysterious terror, and back to wilderness survival.

Mind over Matter

While many adventurous activities can be costly and difficult for a beginner to get into, backcountry camping is an exception. Not much equipment is needed, and the most expensive gear—including tents and bedding—rarely needs to be replaced. Top-of-the-line shelters and sleeping bags can be pricey, but quality used items can often be found online or at rummage sales. Some people buy the equipment for one trip and never plan to camp again!

Also, novice campers needn't be too worried about their physical prowess. While many of the survival experts seen on TV are men in impressive physical shape, backcountry camping is manageable by both males and females of all ages and fitness levels. Stamina and strength are definitely helpful in many circumstances, but a successful backcountry outing generally has more to do with preparedness, resourcefulness, and attitude than it does with natural athleticism or physical ability.

Some physical conditioning is wise and falls under the category of preparedness. Campers should be well-practiced in their given mode of travel before going on an extended camping trip. Developing blisters from walking, sore muscles from rowing, or a sore backside from a bike seat or saddle on the first day of a multi-day outing can make for an unpleasant experience.

Another aspect of preparedness is selecting equipment to bring or leave behind. Bring too much, and it will become too heavy to haul around. But bring too little, and you may not be able to adapt to changing weather conditions, handle emergencies, start fires, prepare meals, or set up camp. It can also mean having to skimp on food and drink. Novice campers do well to err on the side of too much rather than too little. After a few trips, experience will have taught them what they

can and can't do without. Remember, though, that every camping experience is different. Just because bug spray and an extra jacket weren't needed on one trip doesn't mean they should be left behind on the next.

Learning some specific skills before going camping also makes a camper better prepared. First-aid courses are helpful, since the nearest medical professionals may be hours or even days away during a camping trip. An **orienteering** class or even online videos can teach a camper how to use maps and compasses more effectively. Videos can also demonstrate which natural materials to look for and how to use them when building campfires. Novice campers should practice some of these fire-starting techniques prior to camping, because a little dampness or lower oxygen levels at high altitudes can make starting a fire much slower than many people expect.

Even if a camper is well prepared, mishaps such as lost or broken equipment or unexpected weather conditions can ruin even the best-laid plans. This is when resourcefulness is needed. A little creativity and materials provided by nature can reinforce a damaged tent or add warmth to inadequate bedding. The position of the sun and stars can provide guidance should a compass fail. Devising ways of collecting rainwater can solve the problem of having too little drinking water.

Fortunately, campers don't have to come up with all

A Mini Sleeping Bag Model

In nature, cold objects draw heat out of warm objects until the temperatures are equal. Sleeping bag insulation has many little air pockets that slow down this transfer of heat, allowing a person to stay warm longer on a cold night. However, if the air pockets are flattened (such as when the bottom of a bag is compressed under a person's body), the insulation won't work. A simple way to model this concept is to put a pair of gloves or mittens on. In one hand, hold an ice cube loosely. In the other, squeeze an ice cube tight, which will compress the insulation. The tight hand will get cold faster, demonstrating why even the best sleeping bags aren't warm if placed directly on cold ground.

One's attitude and general belief that a bad situation can turn out well is critical for anyone who plans to go camping.

their own solutions on the fly. Pocket-sized survival books show how to deal with many unexpected events. Before heading out on a trip, look through such a book, so vital information can be found and applied more quickly if needed. Also, if the book itself is lost or ruined somehow, campers will need to fall back on their own knowledge.

Finally, one's attitude and general belief that a bad situation can turn out well is critical for anyone who plans to go camping. This can mean maintaining hope and clear thinking in a life-or-death survival situation, but it also applies to common inconveniences that all campers face. The person who gripes about minor soreness, mosquito bites, or being a little too warm or too cool is not cut out for camping. Nor is the person who demands a plush bed, hot running water, and modern restroom facilities. Campers who panic every time a rain cloud rolls in will be severely limited as to when and where they camp.

T his does not necessarily mean that frequent campers *enjoy* bug bites, achy muscles, major temperature swings, or sleeping on the hard ground. But they find that the pros of camping—natural surroundings, pleasant scenery, and simplified lifestyle, to name a few—outweigh the cons. The risks and challenges presented by nature help put

Outfitters who lead climbs up Mt. Everest have several designated campsites along the multi-day climb. The highest of these can be nearly five miles (8 km) above sea level.

modern complaints and worries into perspective. And the temporary inconveniences of camping often help people prioritize what's really important when they get back to their daily lives.

Then there are those rare individuals who simply get a thrill from camping. They enjoy hunkering down in nasty weather, sleeping amid coyote calls, and generally adapting to whatever Mother Nature conjures up. They aren't bothered when a tent pole breaks. They might not even bring a tent to begin with. Covering themselves in mud seems to them a sensible form of insect repellent, and a freshly caught trout cooked over a campfire—started with dried **fungi**—may please them more than the finest restaurant dinner. It is these types of people who take the common recreation of camping and turn it into an extreme adventure.

Glossary

arachnid   a class of animals including spiders, scorpions, ticks, and mites; usually having two distinct body segments and eight legs

backcountry   an area that is away from developed or populated areas

car camping   a form of camping in which people can park their vehicles in or very near their campsites

foliage   a collective grouping of plant life, especially leafy branches, plants, and flowers

freeze-dried   referring to food or other substances that are frozen and then have water molecules removed by altering the pressure around the substance

fungi   members of a kingdom of somewhat plant-like organisms that often grow on or feed off of other organic material; they include mold and mushrooms

hominids   primate mammals that usually walk on two legs; refers to humans and extinct human ancestors

mountaineers   people who climb mountains for sport or recreational purposes

mushers   people who manage and guide dog sled teams, especially in dog sled races

orienteering	an activity in which people use a map and compass to find their way through an unfamiliar area
three-season	referring to outdoor equipment designed for use in three seasons: spring, summer, and fall; usable but not optimal for winter

Selected Bibliography

Back, Joe. *Horses, Hitches, and Rocky Trails*. New York: Skyhorse, 2013.

Curtis, Rick. *The Backpacker's Field Manual: A Comprehensive Guide to Mastering Backcountry Skills.* New York: Three Rivers Press, 2005.

Gerke, Randy. *Outdoor Survival Guide*. Champaign, Ill.: Human Kinetics, 2010.

Jacobson, Cliff. *Canoeing and Camping Beyond the Basics*. 3rd ed. Guilford, Conn.: FalconGuides, 2007.

McManners, Hugh. *The Backpacker's Handbook*. New York: Dorling Kindersley, 1995.

National Geographic Guide to the National Parks of the United States. 6th ed. Washington, D.C.: National Geographic Society, 2009.

Sweeney, Michael S. *National Geographic Complete Survival Manual*. Washington, D.C.: National Geographic Society, 2008.

Tawrell, Paul. *Wilderness Camping & Hiking*. Lebanon, N.H.: Exxa LLC, 2007.

Websites

Camping-Field-Guide.com
www.camping-field-guide.com

This website covers a wide range of camping topics, from fun gift and game ideas to instructions on tying knots, identifying animal tracks, selecting critical equipment, and planning a trip.

Outdoor Gear Lab
www.outdoorgearlab.com

This site provides independent evaluations of tents, sleeping bags and pads, stoves, lanterns, and other camping essentials. Although they cannot review every available product, their write-ups give ideas of what features to look for.

Note: Every effort has been made to ensure that any websites listed above were active at the time of publication. However, because of the nature of the Internet, it is impossible to guarantee that these sites will remain active indefinitely or that their contents will not be altered.

Index

American Indians 14
backcountry camping 29–31, 32, 33–34,
    39–42, 44–46, 47, 66–67
bivouac sacks 34
campfires 20, 34, 42, 46, 49, 50, 68, 71,
    76
car camping 28–29
cowboys 17, 60
cultural influences 53–55, 58, 59–62,
    64–65, 67
    literature 54, 55, 58, 59, 61
    television and films 54, 60–62, 64, 67
Defoe, Daniel 54
drinking water 37, 71
equipment 19, 25, 26, 28, 30, 31, 66, 68,
    71
first-aid kits 30, 40–41
food 20, 28–29, 34, 37, 42, 44, 68, 76
    freeze-dried meals 34, 37
    s'mores 20
Grylls, Bear 62
hominids 12
London, Jack 59
McCandless, Christopher 64
McManus, Patrick F. 58
national parks 18, 29, 47
    Grand Canyon 18
    Yellowstone 18
    Yosemite 18
navigation 28, 39–40, 70, 71
    Global Positioning System (GPS)
        39–40
    orienteering 70
organizations and clubs 19
    Boy Scouts of America 19
plants 14, 42, 64
risks 32, 39–42, 44–45, 47, 62, 67, 68,
    71, 74
Search and Rescue (SAR) 47
shelter 12, 13–14, 17, 19, 20, 22, 25–26,
    28, 30, 32, 33–34, 45–46, 49–50,
    66, 71
    camper trailers 20, 25–26

covered wagons 17
recreational vehicles (RVs) 17, 20,
    25–26
tents 14, 17, 20, 22, 26, 28, 30, 32,
    33–34, 49, 66
tepees 14
sleeping bags 20, 28, 34, 49, 66, 72
Stroud, Les 62
Tolkien, J. R. R. 59
Treadwell, Timothy 64–65
Twain, Mark 55
weather 17, 18, 28, 32, 33, 45, 47, 68, 71,
    76
wildlife 41, 44–45, 64